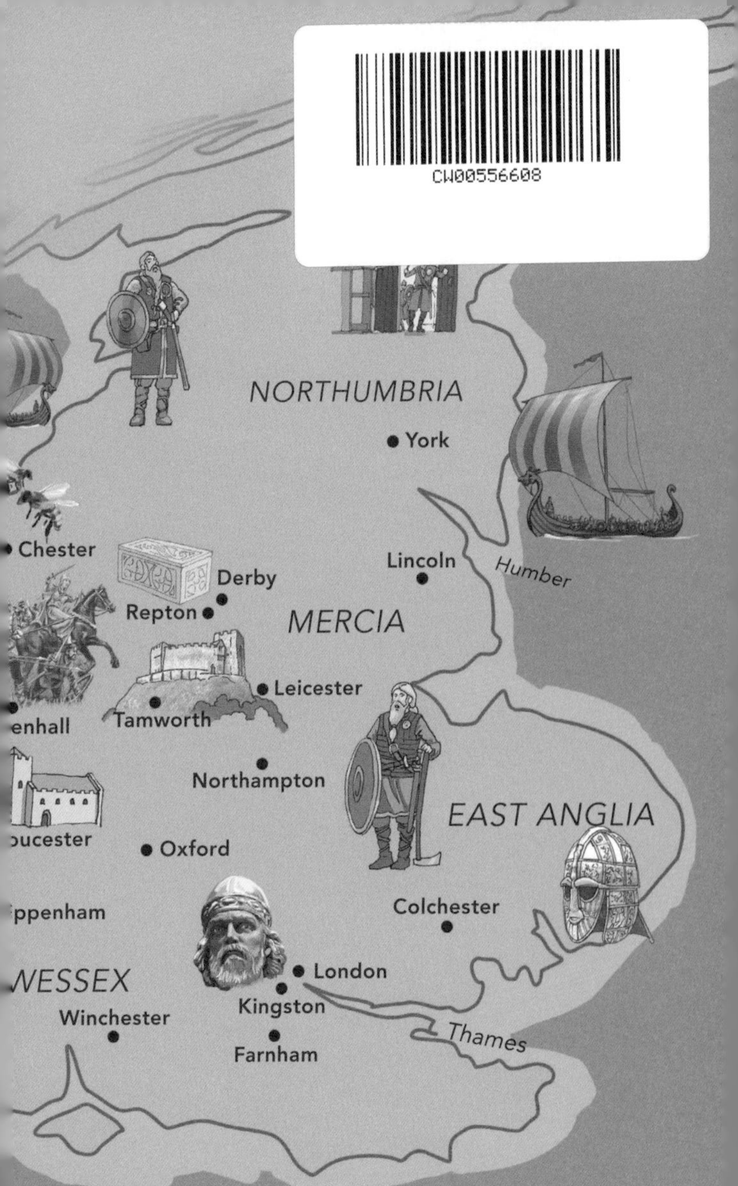
CW00556608
NORTHUMBRIA
York
Chester
Lincoln
Humber
Derby
Repton
MERCIA
Leicester
Tamworth
enhall
Northampton
EAST ANGLIA
oucester
Oxford
ppenham
Colchester
London
WESSEX
Kingston
Winchester
Thames
Farnham

Series 117

This is a Ladybird Expert book, one of a series of titles for an adult readership. Written by some of the leading lights and outstanding communicators in their fields and published by one of the most trusted and well-loved names in books, the Ladybird Expert series provides clear, accessible and authoritative introductions, informed by expert opinion, to key subjects drawn from science, history and culture.

Every effort has been made to ensure images are correctly attributed; however, if any omission or error has been made please notify the Publisher for correction in future editions.

MICHAEL JOSEPH

UK | USA | Canada | Ireland | Australia
India | New Zealand | South Africa

Michael Joseph is part of the Penguin Random House group of companies whose addresses can be found at global.penguinrandomhouse.com

Penguin
Random House
UK

First published 2019

001

Printed in Italy by L.E.G.O. S.p.A.

A CIP catalogue record for this book is available from the British Library
ISBN: 978–0–718–18826–9

www.greenpenguin.co.uk

Penguin Random House is committed to a sustainable future for our business, our readers and our planet. This book is made from Forest Stewardship Council® certified paper.

Æthelflæd

England's Forgotten Founder

Tom Holland

with illustrations by
Colin Shearing

Ladybird Books Ltd, London

On 12 June 918, the most celebrated woman of her age died. Today, few remember Æthelflæd. No one in English history, though, has been more unjustly forgotten. The daughter, sister and aunt of great kings, she was a ruler as remarkable as any of them. She founded cities, she sponsored learning, and she defeated the enemies of her people. Her achievements would prove enduring. It was on the foundations laid by Æthelflæd that a new kingdom, in the decades following her death, would come to be built – a kingdom that lasts to this day. England owes much to her founding mother.

Why has Æthelflæd faded into oblivion? In part, no doubt, it is because she is a shadowy figure. We do not know nearly as much about her as we would like. But there is another reason as well. England is the oldest nation state in Europe. The country seems such a fixture that it is tempting to think that it was always bound to come into existence. But things might have been very different. The fashioning of a united kingdom of 'Englalonde' was not inevitable. The challenges that confronted Æthelflæd and her father – the king we commemorate as Alfred 'the Great' – were formidable. Fearsome enemies had to be defeated, and the fragments of ancient realms soldered together. Peoples with distinct and proud traditions had to be brought to share a common identity. A nation had to be forged.

It was an astonishing feat of state-building – the most decisive in British history. The story of Æthelflæd is the story of how it came to be achieved.

Æthelflæd was born in 870, to a father of royal stock. Alfred was the younger brother and presumptive heir of the King of Wessex, a realm centred in the south of Britain. The line was an ancient one. The kings of Wessex claimed descent from a Saxon adventurer named Cerdic, who was said to have landed in Britain some eighty years after the collapse of Roman rule. Other, more distant ancestors included Woden, the king of the gods. Æthelflæd's pedigree was one that linked her to the very beginnings of her people.

The Saxons, though, were not alone in having crossed the North Sea and founded kingdoms in what had once been Roman Britain. A people called the Angles had done the same. Some had settled in the east of the island, in the land that became known as 'East Anglia'. Another Anglian kingdom, Mercia, lay directly north of Wessex, and a third, Northumbria, stretched from the Humber all the way to the Firth of Forth. For centuries, these various kingdoms had maintained an uneasy coexistence, sometimes fighting one another, sometimes patching up alliances. Borders were rarely stable, and smaller kingdoms, over the course of the centuries, had increasingly been absorbed into the territory of larger ones. This was how Kent and Sussex, both of them originally independent, had ended up ruled by the kings of Wessex. By the time of Æthelflæd's birth, West Saxon power had come to embrace the whole of the south of Britain.

Kingship was a tough business. Only rulers proficient in battle could hope to survive. The ancestors cherished by Anglo-Saxon kings were those who had fought and won great victories. This was why – although Æthelflæd was Alfred's eldest child – she had no prospect of succeeding him. War was seen as men's work.

The ultimate basis of power was always military might. The supreme duty of any king was the defence of his people from incursions by rival warlords. Ravaging was a constant threat. Invaders would aim to seize all they could. If crops were devastated – as they often were – then starvation would invariably threaten. As peasants died of hunger, magnates would suffer from the impoverishment of their holdings, and a king might find his prestige mortally threatened. Only by leading his warriors on a reprisal raid, by seizing enough gold to become a byword for generosity, a ring-giver, could he hope to repair the damage.

Victory was best assured by fighting with the ferocity and cunning of a natural predator. Warriors would don helmets crested with boars, and wear their swords in scabbards decorated with serpents or hawks. Marching to war, an army would invariably be tracked by flocks of ravens. Deep within the forbidding darkness of the forests, wolves might well be heard, howling with anticipation at the feast to come. After the slaughter, the corpses of the defeated would be left as food for the 'beasts of battle'. Later, once the campaign had been brought to a close, poets would salute them. '"But now start war," the carrion-birds shall sing. The grey-cloaked wolf shall yell, the spear resound.'

Æthelflæd might not have been raised to the practice of arms – but no daughter of a king could have failed to learn from song, of the glory and the horror of war.

There was more to ruling Wessex, though, than winning battles. Its kings also had a duty to Christ. The days of worshipping Woden were long gone. Although he continued to feature in their kings' lineage, he did so now as a mortal hero, not as a god. Æthelflæd was born into a dynasty that had been Christian for two centuries. Her father, for all his renown as a warrior, was also famously devout. Naturally, then, Alfred did not hesitate to have his first child baptised.

The great model of a Christian kingdom, though, was not Wessex but Northumbria. Renowned for the holiness of its monasteries and the learning of its scholars, it had also been ruled by a much revered warrior saint. Oswald, the son of a fallen Northumbrian king, had returned from exile in 634, at a time when the future of Christianity in Northumbria was still hanging in the balance. Cornered by his enemies, he had first fashioned a huge wooden cross, and then led his outnumbered forces to a crushing victory. For eight triumphant years he had been the most powerful ruler in Britain. It was under his rule that Northumbria had become decisively Christian. Then, defeated by a pagan king of Mercia, Oswald had been killed and hacked to pieces. Some decades later, portions of his dismembered corpse had been laid to rest near Lincoln, in an abbey named Bardney. The night before they were buried, a miraculous beam of light had been seen rising from the coffin. Oswald's remains had cured fevers and banished evil spirits. Such was the blaze of his reputation that his memory came to be cherished as reverently in Wessex as it was in Northumbria.

Ruin, though, had come to the kingdoms of the Angles. In 793, fiery dragons had been seen in the skies over Northumbria. Shortly afterwards, pirates from Scandinavia had descended on Lindisfarne, the kingdom's most celebrated monastery, and sacked it. This catastrophe had been a portent of worse to come. For decades, raiders in their dragon ships had continued to sail across the North Sea and bleed Northumbria dry. 'Wicingas', their victims called them: 'robbers'. Then, in 867, the wicingas – the Vikings – delivered the death blow. York, the richest entrepôt in Britain, was captured. Two of Northumbria's kings were killed. Anglian rule was ended. Viking warlords carved up the lands once ruled by Saint Oswald.

Two years later, it was the turn of another Anglian kingdom to be overrun. In 869, a great Viking army embarked on a great ravage across East Anglia. When Edmund, the King of the East Angles, met the invaders in battle, he was defeated. Some said that he fell in battle; others that he was taken prisoner, and then, when he refused to renounce Christ, shot dead with arrows. Whatever the truth, one thing was certain: East Anglia, like Northumbria, had been crushed. Another once-independent kingdom had been brought under Viking rule.

Such were the circumstances into which Æthelflæd was born. They could hardly have been more perilous. Of the realms ruled by Anglian and Saxon kings, only two now remained: Mercia and Wessex. Old enemies, they knew that they had little choice but to combine against the common foe.

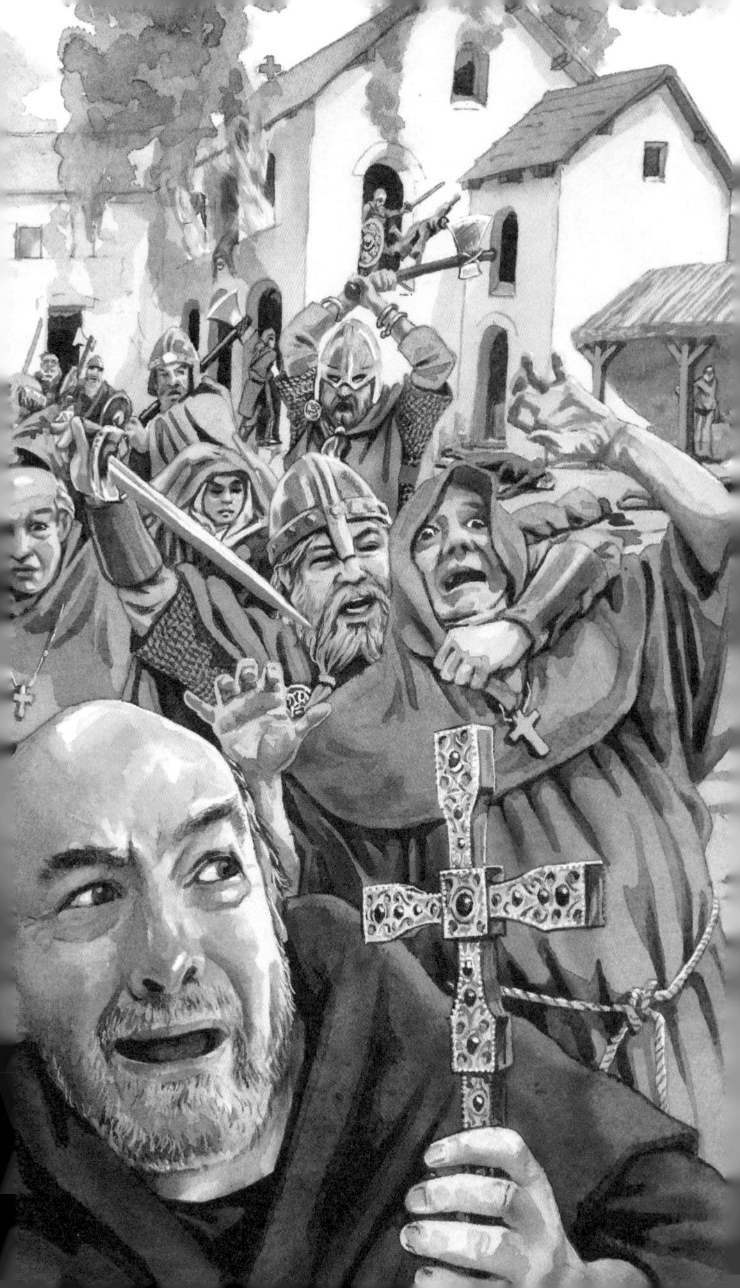

Æthelflæd herself was a living symbol of the alliance between the two kingdoms. Alfred's wife, Ealhswith, was a Mercian, and so their daughter had Anglian as well as Saxon blood flowing in her veins. The couple had married in 868, even as Northumbria was being dismembered. This had provided a backdrop more than menacing enough to concentrate the minds of Mercians and West Saxons alike.

Then, in 871, Alfred's brother died, and Alfred succeeded to the throne. Grimly aware that his people faced a life-or-death struggle, he did all that he could to forge a common front with Burgred, the Mercian king. The Viking tide, though, was rising. The eastern stretches of Mercia were increasingly slipping from Burgred's control. In 874, an invasion force struck at the very heart of his kingdom. The fall of Repton, where the kings of Mercia lay buried in the crypt of the church, was a devastating humiliation. As the Vikings set up their winter quarters in the town, Burgred fled into exile.

Mercia's fate was sealed. The installation of a puppet king on the vacant throne fooled no one. By 877, a Viking army had seized Gloucester, in the far south-west of the kingdom. Other warbands appeared along the line of the Thames. They were now on the very doorstep of the last surviving Anglo-Saxon kingdom. Northumbria, East Anglia, Mercia – all had fallen. That winter, Alfred could only pray that Wessex would not be next.

In the event, so swiftly did the crisis come that Alfred found himself ambushed by it. On the twelfth night after Christmas, he and his court were at the royal residence of Chippenham. Not only was it the dead of winter but a truce had been signed by the Vikings. Alfred had no reason to expect an attack. That was why, when it came, it took him utterly by surprise. As Chippenham was pillaged, he fled into the night.

The future of Wessex, and of Æthelflæd with it, was now hanging by a thread. Giving his pursuers the slip, Alfred took refuge in the marshes of Somerset. Athelney, 'the island of the princes', was a fastness so mired around by lagoons as to be impregnable: an ideal hiding place. Alfred, though, was not content to skulk. Instead, he built a fort, and set to rallying his demoralized subjects. That May, he rode out from Athelney. Meeting with the Vikings in battle, he won a decisive victory. The survivors of the slaughter, fleeing to Chippenham and holing up inside its walls, were starved into submission. Guthrum, the Viking war-leader, accepted baptism. He and his followers agreed to withdraw to East Anglia. Alfred's victory had saved Wessex.

A further treaty, agreed a year or so later, divided Mercia into two. The eastern half of the kingdom was annexed by Guthrum; the western half came under the effective control of Alfred.

Æthelflæd, still only ten years old, may not have paid much attention to these negotiations – but they were destined to change her life.

'Success in warfare, yes – but also in wisdom.' Here was Alfred's manifesto. Tireless though he was as a warrior, he was also committed to the arts of peace. He looked back with nostalgia to a time when Wessex had been dotted with monasteries, each one a radiant beacon of learning. His commitment to reviving this golden age was whole-hearted. Scholars from far afield were invited to his court. Exhausting though the duties of kingship were, he even found time to work on translations from Latin himself.

Unsurprisingly, then, Alfred was keen that his children be brought up to value learning. His second child, Edward – who had been born some four years after Æthelflæd – was an obvious focus of his attentions. After all, as his heir presumptive, the boy needed to be given an education worthy of a king. Alfred, though, was determined that his daughters should be equally well educated. At court, they were instructed by both male and female tutors. They were taught to read scripture and poetry, and trained in the virtues appropriate to a royal court. As a result, Æthelflæd grew up very much her father's daughter: learned, devout and martial in her ambitions.

This was just as well. Æthelflæd was as important to Alfred's plans as Edward. If his son's destiny was to rule as King of Wessex, then his eldest daughter's lay beyond the bounds of her native land, to the north.

The time was fast approaching when Æthelflæd would leave for Mercia . . .

Alfred, whose sagacity as a leader was unrivalled, knew that he had to tread carefully with the Mercians. Their suspicion of West Saxon ambitions ran too deep to permit him to rule them directly as their king. The overlordship of western Mercia that he had secured as a result of his treaty with Guthrum was a precarious and ambivalent thing. He certainly could not afford to jeopardize it by scorning Mercian sensitivities.

Fortunately, Alfred was patently fond of Mercians. His own wife, Ealhswith, was one, and so too was Plegmund, a distinguished scholar whom he appointed Archbishop of Canterbury. As a result, he was able to present himself to the Mercians as a ruler familiar with their customs and respectful of their traditions. Rather than impose a West Saxon prince on them, he opted instead to forge an alliance with the most powerful man in Mercia. Æthelred had first emerged as the kingdom's dominant nobleman in succession to the Vikings' toppled puppet king. Graced by Alfred with the title of subregulus – 'sub-king' – he was known in Mercia itself as 'Myrcna Hlaford' – 'Lord of the Mercians'. The ambivalence was no doubt deliberate.

It certainly served Alfred's purposes. By giving Æthelflæd as a bride to the much older Æthelred, he was able to bestow on his eldest daughter an almost queenly dignity. The marriage proved a great success. Not only was Æthelred bound by it more closely to Alfred's dynastic ambitions but Æthelflæd proved more than equal to the task of winning her new subjects' hearts.

Half-Mercian herself, she was embraced by them as one of their own.

In the autumn of 899, after a long and heroic reign, Alfred finally breathed his last. He died confident in the knowledge that his two eldest children had served a worthy apprenticeship. Edward was in his mid-twenties when he succeeded to the throne of Wessex and was already a seasoned warrior. In 893, when a vast Viking warband landed on West Saxon shores, Alfred had left it to his son to deal with the crisis. Edward had shown himself fully deserving of such confidence. Falling on the invaders at Farnham, he had roundly defeated them and then harried the survivors across the Thames. The new King of Wessex understood what it took to serve as the shield of his people.

So too did his sister. It was not only West Saxons who had fought at Farnham. Mercians had also joined in the slaughter. Æthelflæd, whose childhood had been so disrupted, so menaced by the threat of invasion, was no less attentive to the need to blunt the Viking threat than her brother. Fortunately, her husband was a man equal to the many challenges that faced Mercia. As well as fighting alongside Edward at Farnham, Æthelred had made sure to patrol his frontier with the Viking-occupied lands to the east: the Danelaw, as they would come to be known. Mercia just like Wessex, was being steeled in the requirements of resistance.

Æthelflæd, as wife of the Lord of the Mercians and sister of the King of Wessex, had a key role to play. No one did more to cement the alliance between their two peoples. She was the embodiment of something novel and momentous: an Anglo-Saxon identity.

But she was also much more. Æthelflæd was not her father's daughter for nothing. She knew that simply defeating the Vikings in battle would be insufficient to set Mercia back on a firm footing; towns had to be redeemed from ruin and oblivion. The settlement lavished with Æthelflæd's particular attentions was Gloucester. Once a Roman city, it had long been a wilderness of weeds and crumbling brick-work, where Viking warbands had found a ready base. On Æthelflæd's orders, the nettles and brambles were cleared, and the city walls repaired. A new street plan was laid out. Markets were established. What had previously been a menacing wasteland was transformed into a wealthy stronghold of Mercian power.

Æthelflæd also made sure to endow Gloucester with a religious foundation of the kind that her father had so valued. It was a mark of her confidence in the security that had been brought to Mercia, that the priory of Saint Peter was founded outside the city walls. Built of brick plundered from a nearby Roman temple, it served as a potent demonstration of Æthelflæd's determination to endow Gloucester with God's favour. But it spoke as well of something more: her passion, inherited from her father, for education. Without flourishing churches and monasteries, there could be no learning; and without learning, there could be no effective administration. Æthelflæd's model of rule was one which depended as much on the issuing of charters as on the practice of arms. Her court, as a result, was one where scholarship was highly prized.

One boy in particular would profit from Æthelflæd's passion for learning. Athelstan was her nephew, the eldest son of Edward and a West Saxon noblewoman named Ecgwynn. Born in either 894 or 895, he had been a great favourite of Alfred, who had invested the young boy with a sword-belt and a richly dyed cloak. Far from securing Athelstan's future, though, his father's succession to the throne of Wessex had placed it in severe jeopardy. The early months of Edward's reign had been gripped by dynastic feuding, and the new king, keen to consolidate his authority, had come to view Ecgwynn as an expendable pawn. Soon enough, she had been set aside. Then, in 901, Edward's new wife bore him a son: Ælfweard. The infant prince was immediately given signal marks of favour. No one doubted that he was now his father's preferred heir. Athelstan's presence in the West Saxon court had become an embarrassment.

So it was that the boy was packed off to Mercia. Neither his mother's humiliation nor his own exile from his father's side impaired Athelstan's determination to prove himself worthy of his pedigree. If anything, it fuelled it. Æthelflæd's court provided her nephew with a fit training ground. Athelstan would grow up a celebrated warrior, but he would also be hailed, even as a young boy, for his devotion both to Christ and to scholarship. 'Abundantly are you endowed with the holy eminence of learning.'

Above all, though, beside his aunt, Athelstan could learn the most invaluable lessons of all: the practical arts required of a ruler.

In Wessex, suspicion of powerful women ran deep. The story was told of one Mercian princess who, after marrying a West Saxon king, had behaved like the worst kind of tyrant: promoting her favourites, destroying her rivals and eventually – albeit by accident – poisoning her husband. As a result, the very title 'queen' had been brought into disrepute. No wife of a West Saxon king was permitted to use it, nor even to sit beside her husband's throne.

In Mercia, though, Æthelflæd's status as Alfred's daughter had provided her with a degree of authority that she would never have been permitted to exercise back in Wessex. Even in the early years of her marriage, charters had been issued on which she featured equally alongside Æthelred. Then, in 900, some began to appear in her name alone. In the years that followed, her grip on power tightened. Æthelred, old and weary, was also increasingly an invalid. Although able on occasion to stir himself, to issue grants of land or to negotiate with Viking ambassadors, in general he found the day-to-day demands of government too much for him. Fortunately, though, in Æthelflæd he had a wife more than capable of picking up the reins.

No woman, in a world as turbulent and violent as that into which Æthelflæd had been born, would ever have been able to govern solely on the strength of her pedigree. Her rule was a tribute above all to her remarkable abilities: to her vision, to her determination and to her capacity to inspire loyalty. Shield of her people, it was she whom the Mercians increasingly trusted to preserve them amid the perils of the age.

The most immediate challenge faced by Æthelflæd lay in the far north of her realm. The sea lanes between Britain and Ireland were filling with dragon ships. In 902, a Viking stronghold by the name of Dublin, which for sixty years had dominated the approaches to the River Liffey, had fallen to two Irish kings, and the entire military elite of the settlement had been expelled. Although their leader had sought refuge in Alba, the realm in the far north of Britain ruled by the King of the Scots, most had made a shorter journey. It was an easy crossing from the Liffey to the western seaboard of Northumbria. There, the conquerors of the ancient Anglian kingdom had put down deep roots. York, filled with goods from as far afield as Russia and Constantinople, was as prosperous as anywhere in the Viking world. Not only that, but its rulers had always had close relations with the Dubliners. The news that land-hungry warbands from across the Irish Sea were arriving in Northumbria and pressing on the northern frontiers of Mercia understandably filled Æthelflæd with alarm.

Her response was twofold. When some Dubliners, led by a Viking named Ingimund, approached her with a request for lands, she obliged by settling them on the Wirral, a protuberance of land bounded on one side by the sea and on the other by the Mersey. Simultaneously, she looked for a way to bottle them up on the peninsula. Fortunately, just south of the Wirral lay the crumbling walls and weed-covered streets of a long-abandoned ghost town: the Roman city of Chester.

In 907, Æthelflæd sent in the builders.

As in Gloucester, so in Chester. Æthelflæd consciously sponsored a programme of urban renewal. Fortifications were repaired, markets set up and a new street plan laid out. A wilderness of ruins that in 892 had provided a Viking warband with a base for its depredations was transformed into the northernmost stronghold of Mercian power.

The refortification of Chester was completed just in time. On the Wirral, Ingimund was getting restless. Tiring of the lands he had been granted by Æthelflæd, he began to look around for fresh pickings. Raising a warband, he advanced on Chester. Tales of what happened next, improved with every retelling, would end up the toast of Ireland. Camping out in front of the city, the Vikings sought to storm it. The defenders, though, refused to be cowed. Boiling beer in cauldrons, they poured it on to their assailants. Even more innovatively, they carried beehives up on to the city walls and dropped them on to the besieging army. 'The attackers,' so one Irish chronicler recorded, 'could not move their legs or hands from the great number of bees attacking them.' Ingimund, abandoning his attempt to capture Chester in the face of these inventive defensive measures, retreated to the Wirral. Æthelflæd, determined not to permit a repeat of this escapade, was soon building fortresses directly along the Mersey. The line of communications between the Irish Sea and York was being systematically throttled.

The impact of these measures was widely felt. Æthelflæd's feats were reported in admiring tones across Wales and Ireland. The glamour of her reputation overseas was coming to possess an increasingly regal lustre. She was, so one Irish chronicler proclaimed, 'the ever renowned Queen of the Saxons'.

To celebrate her refounding of Chester, Æthelflæd had a coin minted that was stamped with a potent image: a tower. A symbol of the fortifications that had enabled the city to defy the Vikings, it served simultaneously as an illustration of a church. No better representation of Æthelflæd's ambitions for Mercia could possibly have been devised. Her father, in the wake of his great victory over Guthrum, had implemented a programme of urban regeneration as the surest way to keep Wessex secure from the Vikings. By founding burhs – towns ringed with fortifications and endowed with marketplaces for the generation of taxes – he had aimed to make his kingdom both impregnable and wealthy. The policy was one that his two eldest children had assiduously followed. Chester was only the northernmost of a line of burhs that, year by year, was coming to extend from the Mersey to the Thames estuary. The frontier that Mercia and Wessex jointly shared with the Danelaw was being rendered proof against any attempt by the Vikings to breach it. Between them, Æthelflæd and Edward were sponsoring the first ever pan-English infrastructure project.

The expense and manpower required were, of course, immense. Sister and brother alike, though, were prepared to look to the long term. The tower stamped on Æthelflæd's coins was a token not just of what she had achieved in Chester but also of her hopes for fusing Mercia and Wessex into a single political entity. With perhaps a quarter of all the adult males in the two kingdoms employed in either constructing or garrisoning the great screen wall of burhs, it served to remind both Angles and Saxons of what they were fast becoming: a single people, united in common purpose.

EA
DY
HD

By 909 the scale of construction along Mercia's eastern flank was such that Æthelflæd felt ready to go on the attack. While Edward led a combined force of West Saxons and Mercians into the Danelaw and ravaged it for a month, his sister contributed to the campaign with an exploit of striking boldness. Heading deep into Viking-held territory, a Mercian task force made straight for the abbey of Bardney. Opening the coffin of Saint Oswald and removing the contents, the Mercians then rode back home in triumph with their prize. The relics were laid to rest in Gloucester, in the recently founded priory of Saint Peter – which, in their honour, was rededicated to Oswald himself.

The feat had achieved two purposes. Firstly, it had taunted the Vikings of the Danelaw with the revelation of Æthelflæd's daring and martial prowess. Secondly – and perhaps, from Æthelflæd's own perspective, more significantly – it had endowed Mercia with the potency of the dead king's charisma. The notion that a saint's relics could provide entire towns with a supernatural security was one that she took for granted. Fortifying Chester, she had made sure to place the body of a Mercian saint in one of its churches, so that the burh's defences would then be touched by the charge of his holiness. Oswald, though, promised protection of an altogether greater order. The presence in Gloucester of Northumbria's most celebrated warrior saint, formidable in battle, devout in his love of Christ, promised to shield the whole of Mercia with the blaze of his radiance.

And this was just as well – for the Vikings, as events would quickly prove, were determined to have their revenge . . .

The counter-blow came a year after Æthelflæd's raid on Bardney. A huge Viking army breached the line of burhs that had been built to try and halt all such invasions and ravaged deep into Mercia, leaving a trail of destruction that extended as far as Wessex. Æthelflæd, refusing to despair, waited for the Vikings to turn back. When they finally did so, they were laden down with plunder and fatally overconfident.

The ambush came while the Vikings were crossing the River Severn near a settlement called Tettenhall. 'Suddenly, squadrons of both Mercians and West Saxons, having formed battle-order, moved against the enemy.' The invaders, taken by surprise, were wiped out in a storm of spears. Three of their kings fell in the slaughter. An entire generation of their warriors was maimed. In earlier, darker times, before the Mercians had been brought to Christ, the site of the battle had been sacred to Woden; but now, with Æthelflæd's warriors enjoying the blessings of victory, the field was reconsecrated to the glory of Saint Oswald.

The Battle of Tettenhall marked a watershed. That three kings had been dispatched 'to the hall of the infernal one' was a measure of just how ambitious the Vikings' war effort had been. Now, though, their power had been decisively broken. Never again would their warbands threaten the farmsteads and fields of Mercia. From now on, with the great line of burhs standing secure, it was Æthelflæd and Edward who would be preparing to launch an invasion.

In 911, a year after the Battle of Tettenhall, Æthelred finally died. Edward, looking to consolidate the frontiers of Wessex, promptly annexed the Thames valley as far as Oxford – but beyond that he did not dare to go. He knew what he owed his sister, and he had no wish to destabilize her. Æthelflæd, long the effective ruler of Mercia, was now formally acknowledged by her subjects as 'Myrcna Hlæfdiga': the 'Lady of the Mercians'.

That a West Saxon should have been hailed as the defender of the 'rights and duties of the Mercian kingdom' was startling enough. That the same West Saxon was also a woman only made Æthelflæd's ability to serve the Mercians as the personification of their identity all the more unprecedented. 'Her rule,' a chronicler recorded, 'was just and lawful.' When the lords of Mercia attended her assemblies, she could hail them as her friends, and mean it. When she presided over legal cases, she could deliver verdicts in the certainty that all would respect her judgement. When she sent armies into the field, she could do so in the confidence that her commands would be obeyed.

In 913, Æthelflæd succeeded in winning a particularly momentous trophy for her people. Tamworth, a town just beyond the frontier in Viking territory, had once been the capital of Mercia, the seat of the kingdom's greatest and most famous rulers. Sacked by the Vikings in 874, its blackened ruins had long served as a standing reproach to the Mercians. Now, at the head of a great army, Æthelflæd crossed the frontier into the Danelaw and took Tamworth back. Restoring it and refortifying it, she consecrated the ancient capital as Mercian once again. It was a feat, so her subjects agreed, that could only have been achieved 'with the help of God'.

Only a woman of remarkable charisma could possibly have done as Æthelflæd did so repeatedly and triumphantly, and stood at the head of victorious campaigns. Advancing on Tamworth, one of her chroniclers proudly reported that, she had gone with 'all the Mercian people'. Although she had not been trained to fight with spear and sword, she would certainly have been raised from childhood to be comfortable in the saddle. Æthelflæd knew the value of being seen by the Mercians – in peace as well as war. There was a tirelessness about her efforts as a ruler that marked her out as Alfred's daughter indeed.

Even though she had restored them herself, she did not keep exclusively to the great centres of Mercia: Gloucester, Chester, Tamworth. Building burhs, constructing defences, she often held court on the very frontiers of her lands. She might celebrate the great feast days on the slopes of hill forts, gazing out into the Danelaw or across to the mountains of Wales. One feast in particular was precious to her, that of the Holy Cross. In her private possession she had a book which described its origin: how, miraculously, the cross on which Christ had suffered death, long lost, had been discovered in Jerusalem. This was the anniversary which Æthelflæd, on 14 September 915, celebrated at a newly founded fort named Weardburh, amid the freshly dug soil of earthworks and the fresh wood of palisades. Long though she had ruled, she never had time to pause.

She knew the test that was approaching – and she intended to be fully prepared.

By 917, the moment long prepared for by Edward and Æthelflæd was finally at hand. Both of them – born as they had been into the firestorm of the Viking attempt to annihilate Wessex – had long since come to a sombre realization: that treaties with such predatory and opportunistic adversaries would never hold. Only by toppling their kings and forcing them at sword point to submit to Anglo-Saxon overlordship would Wessex and Mercia ever enjoy true security. Now, with both kingdoms impregnably lined by a great shield-wall of burhs, the chance was there to crush the Danelaw once and for all.

It was the Vikings themselves who served up the opportunity. When Edward, copying his sister's strategy at Tamworth, planted a burh deep inside the Danelaw and then seized a fortress, the Vikings sought to roll back the advancing line of fortifications by going on the attack. Their raids, though, proved aimless and ineffective. Edward, launching an invasion himself, was altogether more disciplined. The King of the Danelaw, cornered in one of his strongholds, was killed when it was stormed. Colchester was captured and its garrison put to the sword. Over the course of the year ever more of East Anglia was brought to submit. Riding out of Northampton, the Viking commander and his men surrendered to Edward, 'and sought to have him as their protector and lord'.

Meanwhile, further north, in the eastern reaches of what had once been Mercia until their annexation by the Vikings almost fifty years before, the Lady of the Mercians was also on the attack. Riding out from behind her line of burhs, she did so in the confidence that she had the measure of her foes at last.

Æthelflæd's target was the ancient Roman fort of Derby, the Vikings' most significant Mercian base. Viking resistance in the town was quickly broken. Although four of Æthelflæd's lords – men 'who were dear to her' – fell in the fighting by the gates, Derby was briskly conquered and the lands around it brought under Mercian rule. It was her greatest triumph and played a key role in ensuring that, by the end of 917, all the Vikings of East Anglia had been brought to submit to her brother.

Æthelflæd did not rest on her laurels. In the new year, she marched on a second Viking stronghold, the town of Leicester, and brought that to submit as well. Her fame and charisma were now freely acknowledged across the entire North. The King of the Scots, in the most northerly extremes of Britain, sought an alliance with her, as did the Cumbrians of Strathclyde, whose kings held sway from the banks of the Clyde down to the Lake District. Æthelflæd's intentions were clear: to crush the Vikings of York within a vice. With almost all of the Danelaw south of the Humber now brought under Anglo-Saxon control, Northumbria was her obvious next target. Indeed, so desperate were some of the Northumbrian lords to pre-empt her next move that they freely offered her their submission. Æthelflæd did not hesitate to accept it.

But time was running out for the Lady of the Mercians. In June, she fell ill. Fittingly, she died in Tamworth, the stronghold which once had been the seat of Mercia's very greatest kings. Æthelflæd, though a West Saxon, more than deserved to be ranked alongside them. No Mercian king had ever done more for his people.

Æthelflæd left a daughter – but there was to be no second Lady of the Mercians. Edward ordered his niece south, to Wessex, and into a nunnery. He also arranged that Æthelflæd's body be taken to Gloucester, rather than being buried in Tamworth or Repton – where it might have provided a focus for Mercian separatism. There it was laid to rest, next to Æthelred, in Saint Oswald's Priory. Now that his sister had died, Edward was resolved to rule her lands directly. Mercia and Wessex were being fused to form a single Anglo-Saxon realm.

Mercian hopes of being ruled by one of their own were not entirely extinguished, though. In 924, when Edward died just south of Chester, his eldest son was by his side. Athelstan, by now almost thirty, had spent all his formative years in Mercia. The Mercians duly hailed him as their king. Meanwhile, in Wessex, the loyalty of the establishment was to Edward's second son, Ælfweard: a prince who had grown up among them and could be relied upon to defend their interests. It seemed, then, with war between the two brothers threatening, that Mercia and Wessex might once again go their separate ways.

It was not to be. Travelling northwards to meet his father's funeral cortège, Ælfweard fell ill at Oxford and died. The West Saxon nobility and clergy – albeit through gritted teeth – accepted Athelstan as king. He was crowned on 4 September 925 at Kingston, on the River Thames, a venue deliberately chosen because it lay on the frontier between Wessex and Mercia. At the ceremony, the archbishop pointedly reminded the congregation that Athelstan had been elected as king of both realms 'pariter' – 'equally'.

Although Æthelflæd had died too soon to reap the full rewards of her policies in the North, Athelstan – who was not just her heir but to all intents and purposes her foster son – made sure not to betray her legacy. In 927, the Viking King of York died. The chain of fortresses built by Æthelflæd along the Mersey helped to ensure that Athelstan was able to march on the city and capture it, before his successor could sail across the Irish Sea, and claim his throne. Later that year, Athelstan met with the kings of Alba and Strathclyde and accepted their submission. Three years after being crowned the ruler of Wessex and Mercia, Athelstan was being hailed as 'Rex Totius Britanniae' – 'King of the Whole of Britain'.

In the event, the Anglo-Saxon hold on the northern reaches of the island proved precarious. In 939, when Athelstan died, the King of the Scots immediately proclaimed his independence. York was reconquered by the Vikings. War even returned to Mercia: Derby, Leicester, Tamworth – all were stormed. Yet the labours of Æthelflæd had been too great not to endure. By 942, Edmund, Athelstan's half-brother and his successor as King of the Anglo-Saxons, had brought all of Mercia back under his rule. In 944, he took back York. Although Viking efforts to wrest back the city would continue for another eight years, by 952 – when the last claimant to its throne fell in battle – the prospect of an independent Northumbria was at an end. Instead, it was the future of 'Englalonde' that now stood secure.

That a woman played a role in England's creation quite as significant as any man's should be better remembered than it is. Æthelflæd's legacy has endured for 1,100 years. It is not too late to pay the Lady of the Mercians the credit that is her due.

Further Reading

Richard Abels *Alfred the Great: War, Kingship and Culture in Anglo-Saxon England* (Longman, 1998)

Joanna Arman *The Warrior Queen: The Life and Legend of Æthelflæd, Daughter of Alfred the Great* (Amberley, 2017)

Asser *Alfred the Great: Asser's* Life of King Alfred *and Other Contemporary Sources* (Penguin, 1983)

Tim Clarkson *Æthelflæd: The Lady of the Mercians* (John Donald, 2018)

Nicholas Higham and D. H. Hill (eds) *Edward the Elder* (Routledge, 2001)

Nicholas Higham and Martin Ryan *The Anglo-Saxon World* (Yale University Press, 2013)

Tom Holland *Athelstan: The Making of England* (Allen Lane, 2016)

George Molyneaux *The Formation of the English Kingdom in the Tenth Century* (Oxford University Press, 2015)

Pauline Stafford *Unification and Conquest: A Political and Social History of England in the Tenth and Eleventh Centuries* (Edward Arnold, 1989)

F. T. Wainwright 'Æthelflæd, Lady of the Mercians' in *Scandinavian England: Collected Papers* (Phillimore, 1975

Michael Wood *In Search of the Dark Ages* (Ariel, 1981)